CANNING & PRESERVING

THE TECHNIQUES, EQUIPMENT, AND RECIPES TO GET STARTED

Michele Harmeling

Adventure Skills Guides

SAVE AND STORE YOUR FAVORITE FOODS

Adventure Skills Guides

Whether you're using a portion of the season's harvest of tomatoes in a pressure canning recipe for marinara sauce or whipping up a quick batch of raspberry jam, canning and preserving are wonderful ways to save money, stay healthy, and prevent food waste.

This guide is a template to help you get started in the world of canning and preserving. Once you start, you'll see just how versatile and rewarding canning and preserving can be. This guide is intended to whet your appetite, pun fully intended, for this rewarding lifetime pursuit.

MICHELE HARMELING

Michele Harmeling is a writer, explorer, and lover of wild and home-canned foods of all kinds. Residing in picturesque Palmer, Alaska, she enjoys hiking, backpacking, botany, foraging for wild mushrooms and edibles, and preserving her finds using a variety of methods. She is also a freelance photographer and teaches a class aptly entitled "Can I Eat This or Will It Kill Me?" through the Palmer Folk School. Her greatest loves are her son, Walker; their dog and cats; and a good pair of slipper socks.

Cover and book design by Jonathan Norberg
Editor: Brett Ortler
Proofreader: Emily Beaumont

Front cover: jar background, more jars, garlic, and tomato: **Cherries/shutterstock.com;** salsa: **sjarrell/shutterstock.com;** peaches: **zoyas/shutterstock.com**

Back cover: **cinocihancagli/shutterstock.com**

All images copyrighted.

Used under license from Shutterstock.com
andreonegin:19; **bjul:** 6; **dragon_fang:** 21; **Stephanie Frey:** 12; **GalinaSh:** 3; **Alla Greeg:** 8a; **Jenn Huls:** 13; **Henk Jacobs:** 18; **kryzhov:** 9a; **Alexandra Lande:** 4; **Lost_in_the_Midwest:** 9b; **margouillat photo:** 17; **Oksana Mizina:** 10; **alicja neumiler:** 16; **P A:** 11; **PeterG:** 5; **Pixiversal:** 20; **Bryan Pollard:** 24; **ricok:** 22; **Elena Schweitzer:** 23; **sjarrell:** 15; **Southern Light Studios:** 7; **Zigzag Mountain Art:** 14

10 9 8 7 6 5 4 3 2 1

Canning & Preserving: The Techniques, Equipment, and Recipes to Get Started
Copyright © 2020 by Michele Harmeling
Published by Adventure Publications, an imprint of AdventureKEEN
330 Garfield Street South, Cambridge, Minnesota 55008
(800) 678-7006
www.adventurepublications.net
All rights reserved
Printed in China
ISBN 978-1-59193-943-6 (pbk.)

WANT TO START CANNING? HERE'S HOW TO BEGIN

Read through the how-to portions of this guide (see pages 3-9) and familiarize yourself with the ways to process food (boiling-water or pressure canning), potential safety hazards (especially when low-acid foods are concerned), and canning best practices.

Acquire the necessary equipment and make sure that it's modern and calibrated.

Assemble the bounty you want to preserve, then find a recipe from a trusted source that's suitable for the food you've chosen (pages 10-24), and double-check that the processing steps/equipment are suitable for the specific food in question, and your elevation.

Once you've canned your goods and ensured that your jars have sealed correctly and are stored safely, enjoy the newfound bounty that canning and preserving provides!

HELPFUL RESOURCES

GO FORTH AND PRESERVE!

The versatility and flavor of home-canned goods cannot be beat! A wealth of resources and innovative recipes exists, from your local library to the Internet, and you have now mastered the basics!

This means you're ready to go forth and preserve your own food.

OTHER RECIPES

As your confidence and canning experience grow, you may wish to can or preserve foods not listed in this guide. Be sure to always use up-to-date, vetted sources when testing new recipes for different foods. Remember that old recipes do not always meet current safety standards, such as adjusting levels of acidity or cook times.

For safety considerations, the cooking recommendations in this guide are drawn from the USDA's official recommendations in the *Complete Guide to Home Canning*, the gold standard on the subject.

ADDITIONAL HELPFUL RESOURCES

To Find Your Elevation, consult the United States Geological Survey's elevation search tool at http://geonames. usgs.gov/pls/gnispublic

For additional recipes and expert advice, consult the following:

The National Center for Home Food Preservation
https://nchfp.uga.edu

Ball's Fresh Preserving Recipe Bank
freshpreserving.com

Better Homes & Gardens. *Complete Canning Guide: Freezing, Preserving, Drying*, Houghton Mifflin, New York: 2015.

DISCLAIMER

Every effort has been made to ensure the accuracy of information throughout this book, and the contents of this publication are believed to be correct at the time of printing. Nevertheless, the publishers cannot accept responsibility for errors or omissions, for changes in instructions given in this guide, or for the consequences of any reliance on the information provided by the same.

There are few things more satisfying than opening a pantry to see rows of brightly colored, neatly labeled cans and jars. Upon opening this easy guide to canning and preserving, you've started the journey to preserving your favorite foods year-round!

This guide is a beginner's best friend, providing easy-to-follow instructions and time-tested, popular recipes.

For the home-canning enthusiast, let the quick guide serve as a comprehensive reference and the perfect tool to have on hand while experimenting with new foods or reinvigorating staples.

How to Use This Guide

Created to help you get started in the world of canning and preserving, this guide is divided into two sections—one with recipes and details on boiling-water canning, and the other dedicated to pressure canning. In each, we provide you with the details to safely prepare a handful of favorite recipes, from apple butter in a boiling-water canner to canned smoked fish in a pressure canner.

With either method, be sure to follow the time and temperature instructions in your recipe! And please remember to read all safety and health-related information, particularly specific instructions for your personal kitchen equipment and type of canner before you begin.

THE BASICS

Two Types of Canning: Boiling-water Canning vs. Pressure Canning

There are two different ways to can and preserve foods. **Boiling-water canning** immerses acidic foods in a bath of boiling water during the canning process. A boiling-water canner looks much like a large pot and can hold several jars at once on its bottom rack. It is suitable only for acidic foods, such as fruit jams, jellies, stone fruit, and pickles. Boiling-water canning brings the temperature to 212 degrees Fahrenheit, water's boiling temperature at sea level.

Unless additional acid is added to them, low-acid foods **must be pressure-canned**. This includes all vegetables, root vegetables, meats and fish, and tomato products, including salsa and spaghetti sauce. A pressure canner traps steam, increasing the temperature inside the canner to at least 240 degrees, a temperature high enough to destroy *Clostridium botulinum*, which causes botulism. Make sure that you follow low-acid recipes to the letter and only use them from vetted sources. (For the purposes of this guide, such trusted sources as the Center for Home Food Preservation, the Ball Fresh Preserving recipe bank, and the author's home-canning experiences themselves have been referenced to ensure accuracy and safety.)

Boiling-water Canners

Boiling-water canners immerse filled jars in boiling water. The jars must be elevated 1-2 inches above the canner's bottom surface; this is accomplished by lowering jars onto a rack, to keep them from coming into contact with excess heat. There are many variants of such canners (and racks) on the market. The

Boiling-water canning is only suitable for acidic foods.

4

ideal boiling-water canner holds up to seven pint jars and enough water to cover the jar tops with one full inch of boiling water.

You can also fashion your own boiling-water canner out of any large pot with a stable, flat bottom, and space enough that your jars do not touch the pot's sides nor tip over. When using an electric stovetop, fit your canner's pot to the heating element by ensuring it is no more than 4 inches wider than the element's circumference.

Pressure Canners

There are two types of pressure canners. Dial-gauge canners use a gauge to show pressure, which can be controlled by adjusting the heat on your stove. Weighted-gauge canners self-adjust by releasing steam. Before operating your pressure canner, carefully read and follow its instructions. It is also important to regularly test your pressure gauges for accuracy. This service is often available via the manufacturer and sometimes through your local cooperative extension service.

Pressure canning is the only way to safely can low-acid foods.

There are several tried-and-true brands of pressure canners on the market. We suggest reading as much as you can on each, then choosing your new pressure canner according to your personal needs. Considerations may include cost, size, and availability.

All American, Presto, Granite Ware, and Mirro are just a few popular brand names.

The Instant Pot Question

The Instant Pot has become a must-have for home cooks wanting to save time while still producing wholesome meals. The most recent models of Instant Pot (Instant Pot Max, Instant Pot Max 9-in-1) have a "canning" feature that is purportedly able to produce canned goods that are safe and properly sealed.

There are no instructions stating that the Instant Pot's canning feature is recommended for pressure canning, despite the labels on the pot itself. There are also no indicators of exact temperature or pressure on any Instant Pot model (each mode is labeled according to type of food, i.e.; Broth/Soup; Poultry; Beans). This makes it nearly impossible to properly monitor food's cooking temperature and pressure, which are the two essential elements of home canning.

Due to its versatile nature and construction, the Instant Pot may not reach a temperature high enough to eradicate bacteria. It is also not possible to regulate the pressure of an Instant Pot as precisely as when using a pressure canner specifically designed for home canning. This is a significant health risk, as botulism toxin in particular may remain after using the Instant Pot's canning mode.

Canning in an Instant Pot may pose a safety risk as well. Because it is not possible to see exact pressure readings, during cooking or during pressure release, you may risk opening the Instant Pot before all steam and pressure have been released. This could result in burns and other injuries.

For these reasons, the author of this guide and the National Center for Home Food Preservation strongly recommend against the use of an Instant Pot for home canning.

A Cooktop Note

If you have an electric smooth-top cooking surface, check with your manufacturer before using a boiling-water canner. This setup can reflect too much heat and could potentially damage your cooking surface.

Your altitude affects the process time needed to safely preserve food; know your elevation and how to adjust your recipes accordingly.

Keep Altitude in Mind

The boiling point of water varies with altitude. At sea level, it's 212 degrees, but at higher elevations, the boiling temperature is lower. This means that you need to account for your area's altitude when canning and preserving. For boiling-water canning, processing times will be extended. For pressure canners, you must apply additional pressure. We've included a fold-out altitude chart for your convenience.

Sterilizing Jars is Not Required

Older canning guides may recommend sterilizing jars and lids. As long as you process your jars for long enough (and take altitude into account), the canning process itself will sterilize your jars. In all of the recipes in this book, we've already adapted the recipes to ensure that jar sterilization occurs during the canning process. For that reason, do not adjust the jar size called for in each recipe without performing your own calculations to establish the process times for your desired altitude/jar size.

Keep Jars Hot

To prevent the glass from cracking or fracturing, jars should always be hot when pouring a hot mixture into them. You can warm jars by running them through the dishwasher, or by heating them in the canner while preparing the recipe.

No Substitutions
Similarly, don't make substitutions to the recipes listed here.

Clean Jars, Clean Products
Whether you're using new jars and lids, or reusing jars (in good condition, with new lids), always clean them with warm, soapy water and rinse well. Dry before using. Glass Mason-style jars are among the most popular options, and they come in a range of sizes.

Packing Methods
Jars may be filled, or packed, using one of two methods.

You can pack the foods raw—this is best for items that won't keep their shape or texture during canning. **Raw packing** is ideal when pickling items, as it helps them maintain a crisp, fresh texture.

Raw packing is best for softer vegetables, such as peas, corn, and carrots.

Hot packing is another method to pack jars; the food in hot-packed items is cooked in water or syrup first. Almost all canned fruits, such as peaches, pears, and apples, obtain the best texture if prepared using this method.

The recipes in this book will instruct you to use the method best suited to each item.

Headspace
Headspace is an amount of empty space between jarred, hot food and the underside of its lid. As food cools in a closed jar, it expands. This expansion varies. Leaving the correct amount of headspace ensures that a strong seal will form.

Knowing the appropriate headspace to allow is key.

This guide includes an amount of headspace specific to each individual recipe. Follow it precisely to make sure your jars seal well!

Before You Start
Before you get started, it's handy to have adequate sink space and to gather all of your ingredients and equipment in one place. You should also read through the instruction manual for your canner and its accessories, and know how to use it.

You'll also want hot pads or a silicone mat on which to cool jars (otherwise, you may burn your countertop/table).

A permanent marker and large mailing labels work well to identify your preserves.

You may also create your own printed labels at home (avery.com is a great place to create your free account and access label templates for a wide variety of uses).

Chill Out

Once you're done canning, your goods need to be cooled; this is true for both those canned in a hot-water bath or a pressure canner. They need to be cooled at room temperature for at least 12 hours before storage.

It is normal for your jar lids to ping or pop while cooling. This is the sound of the jar lid sucking down in a vacuum. This sound does not indicate that the jars have sealed well, however, so always be certain that you follow the recipe exactly, make adjustments as necessary for your altitude, and carefully inspect your jar seals after cooling.

Checking Jar Seals

A jar's seal is what prevents bacteria from getting inside the jar, and a jar with a failed seal has not safely preserved your items. When examining jars, there should be no "give" in the sealed lid of a properly canned product. To check, press on the middle of the jar with your index finger. If it springs back up when you release your finger, the seal has failed. Another way to check is to look carefully at the jar lid; a well-sealed lid is concave (curves inward).

Jar Failures

Inspect your jars carefully before canning, especially if you are reusing jars. There may be small cracks or chips in jar rims that will prevent lids from properly sealing. Should you notice a failed seal, you may re-process the jar by using a new lid and processing exactly as instructed in the original recipe. This must be done within 24 hours to avoid contamination.

If you see evidence of spoiled food, do not taste or ingest it!

Identifying Spoiled Food

When opening canned items, inspect your jars for evidence of failed seals and spoilage. Before opening, this may be obvious if a jar's seal "button" flexes or gives when touched, liquid is seeping around the lid edge, there appear to be bubbles inside the jar, or food appears discolored.

Discard any suspected spoiled foods immediately. Do not taste or ingest foods from jars you suspect have gone bad!

Spoiled Low-Acid Foods

Spoiled low-acid foods, including all vegetables, along with root vegetables, meats and fish, and tomato products, are a special concern, as they potentially lead to botulism. One can ingest the botulinum toxin by eating spoiled products, or through the skin. Low-acid foods don't necessarily spoil in the same obvious ways (mold, etc.), so if you find a jar of low-acid food that is leaking, with a seal that's failed, or with liquid that spurts out when you open it, consider it contaminated.

If you can low-acid foods and they spoil, experts recommend decontaminating the area.

In such cases, the National Center for Home Food Preservation recommends putting on gloves and sterilizing the spoiled jars and their contents by covering them in water in a large covered pot and boiling for at least 30 minutes before disposing of the jars and food in the trash. After that they also recommend washing your gloved hands and then sanitizing areas where spoiled foods spilled with a solution of one part bleach and five parts water, letting it stand for half an hour, cleaning up any spillage with paper towels, and then re-bleaching the surfaces again, discarding all gloves and paper towels that came into contact with the area of the spoiled food. For the full instructions, visit: https://nchfp.uga.edu/how/store/store_home_canned.html

Storing Preserves: A Full Pantry is a Happy Place

After jars have cooled for 12-24 hours, wipe lids and jars with a damp cloth to remove any food.

Once jars are sealed and cooled, it is not necessary to leave rings in place. Remove the rings if so desired before storing, and save them for future use.

Your preserves will keep best if stored in a cool, dry place away from direct sunlight. Room

Bright preserves are a welcome sight in the dark days of winter.

temperature or just below is ideal, and remember to avoid storing home-canned items near heat sources.

Don't forget to rotate! Place jars closest to reaching their use-by date in front of newer ones, checking periodically for expired foods, or those that must be used soon. Properly sealed, carefully stored foods remain edible for approximately a calendar year.

EASY APPLE BUTTER

Makes approximately 4 pints

Tart apples with a firm texture produce the best results for this slightly spicy spread that makes a rich alternative to jam or jelly (adapted from the National Center for Home Food Preservation's Apple Butter recipe.)

Ingredients:

8 pounds apples of your choice
2 cups prepared apple cider
2 cups white vinegar
2¼ cups granulated sugar
2¼ cups brown sugar, packed

2 tablespoons ground cinnamon
1 tablespoon ground cloves
¾ teaspoon nutmeg
1 teaspoon ground allspice
1 teaspoon salt

Preparation: Rinse apples; remove stems and core. Cut unpeeled apples into quarters. Bring apple cider to a boil in a large pot over medium-high heat. Add vinegar and apple slices.

Cover pot, reduce heat to medium-low and simmer 30 minutes or until apples are soft. Remove from heat. Ladle apples and liquid into a food mill or sieve over a pot, forcing pulp through. Discard remaining skin and seeds. Stir sugars and next 5 ingredients into apple pulp. Simmer over medium-low heat 1 to 2 hours or until thickened and smooth, stirring often to prevent scorching. Keep apple butter hot. Test for doneness by piling a small amount on a plate or spoon. If apple butter holds it shape and no halo of liquid forms around the edge, then it's ready to can.

Prepare boiling-water bath canner. Pack hot apple butter into hot jars, leaving ¼ inch of headspace. Remove air bubbles; wipe jar rims. Cover at once with metal lids, and screw on rings. Process in boiling-water canner for the appropriate time for your altitude.

EASY DILL PICKLES

Makes approximately 7–9 pint jars

Pouring the whole spices used in the pickling brine into each jar of these crispy pickles makes them just as pretty as they are tasty (adapted from the National Center for Home Food Preservation's Quick Fresh-Pack Dill Pickles).

Ingredients:

8 pounds pickling cucumbers (3–5 inches long)

1¼ cups pickling salt, divided

2 gallons water

1½ quarts white vinegar (5%)

¼ cup granulated sugar

2 quarts water

2 tablespoons whole mixed pickling spice (whole coriander, whole black peppercorns, mustard seed, allspice)

4½ tablespoons dill seed (about 1½ teaspoons whole dill seed per jar)

Preparation: Wash cucumbers. Cut off both ends and inspect for blemishes. Dissolve ¾ cup pickling salt in 2 gallons water. Add cucumbers to mixture and let it sit for 12 hours. Drain carefully.

Combine vinegar, sugar, remaining ½ cup pickling salt, and 2 quarts water. Place pickling spice in a clean spice bag and add to the mix. Bring to a boil. Keep hot. Remove spice bag, but don't empty it.

Sprinkle 1½ teaspoons dill seed into each hot jar. Loosely pack cucumbers, filling to ½ inch from top. Cover cucumbers with boiling pickling syrup, transferring some of the remaining whole spices into each jar. Remove air bubbles; wipe jar rims. Cover at once with metal lids, and screw on rings. Process for the appropriate time for your altitude.

BLUEBERRY JAM

Makes approximately 6 half pints

Ever a favorite, this blueberry jam uses pectin to ensure the proper thickness. Popular pectin brands include Ball Realfruit, Sure-Jell, or Fresh-Jell. We recommend dried, powdered pectin in this recipe, as it produced the best results.

Ingredients:

2 pounds fresh blueberries (4 cups)

3 tablespoons bottled lemon juice

4½ tablespoons fruit pectin of your choice (powdered)

5 cups granulated sugar

Preparation: Rinse and drain blueberries. Pick over, removing any stems and leaves and any berries that appear dried out. Carefully crush berries about a cup at a time—a potato masher gives good consistency.

Combine blueberries and lemon juice in large saucepan. Slowly stir pectin into berries.

Bring mixture to a full, rolling boil. Boil on high for 1 minute, stirring constantly.

Add entire amount of sugar, then stir until sugar is dissolved. Boil for 1 minute, stirring constantly.

Pack hot jam into clean hot jars, filling to ¼ inch from top. Remove air bubbles; wipe jar rims. Cover at once with metal lids and screw on rings. Tighten rings until finger-tight. Process in a boiling-water bath for the appropriate time for your altitude. Remove and let cool.

CANNED PEACHES

**Approximately 10 pounds of fresh peaches
(8–9 pints of canned product)**

These golden peaches are preserved in a light syrup and will remind you of summer each time you open a jar! Select ripe peaches, exactly as you would buy to eat raw.

Ingredients:
10 pounds fresh, ripe golden
    peaches (don't use
    white peaches)

For light syrup:
1½ cups granulated sugar
5¾ cups water
Optional: 3-4 tablespoons whole
    dried cloves, to be added to syrup

Preparation: Boil a large pot of fresh, clean water. Prepare an ice bath by filling a large mixing bowl with ice and cold, clean water.

Quickly blanch each peach by placing in boiling water until skins begin to curl. Then dip peaches in ice water. Peel off and discard remaining skins. Cut peaches in half and remove pits. You may cut peaches into slices or simply leave halved.

Combine sugar and 5¾ cups water in a large pot; heat, stirring constantly until sugar dissolves. Keep syrup hot. Loosely pack peaches in hot jars. Cover peaches with hot syrup, filling to ½ inch from top. Remove air bubbles; wipe jar rims. Cover at once with metal lids, and screw on rings until finger-tight. Process in a boiling-water canner for the appropriate time for your altitude.

Note: *Try adding whole cloves to syrup as it boils, for a spicy variation on traditional canned peaches!*

PICKLED BEETS

Approximately 7–8 pounds of small ("baby") beets yields about 8 pints
Adapted from the USDA's recipe for Pickled Beets, this is a slightly sweet, earthy recipe perfect for eating on its own or added to another dish.

Ingredients:

7 pounds small (2-2½ inches),
    fresh beets
4 cups vinegar (5%)
1½ teaspoons pickling salt

2 cups granulated sugar
2 cups water
2 whole cinnamon sticks
12 whole cloves

Preparation: Cut off the tops of the beets, but leave an inch or so of the stem/roots, as this will prevent the beet color from bleeding. Wash the beets, and then sort them by size.

Place beets (grouped by size) and water to cover in a large pot; bring to a boil, and cook 30 minutes or until tender. Drain beets and discard cooking liquid, as it may not be used for canning. Let beet cool; trim off root/stem ends. Gently peel off skins and discard. Cut beets into ¼-inch slices.

Combine vinegar, pickling salt, sugar, and 2 cups water. Add whole cinnamon and cloves to mixture, and bring to a boil. Add the beets to the mix and then allow to simmer for 5 minutes. Remove spices. Ladle cooked beets into hot jars, filling to ½ inch from top. Cover beets with hot pickling liquid, filling to ½ inch from top. Remove air bubbles; wipe jar rims. Cover at once with metal lids, and screw on rings until finger-tight. Process in boiling-water canner for the appropriate time for your altitude.

BEST GAME DAY SALSA

Makes approximately 3 pints

You can't go wrong with chips and salsa for snacks or parties! Can a batch of this crowd-pleasing recipe and impress your friends anytime. Choose a cooking pot that won't react to the high acidity of this recipe. Finely chopping chiles and peppers eliminates the need to remove skins.

Safety Note: *When working with peppers, wear gloves and don't touch your eyes! Wash your hands thoroughly after making this recipe.*

Ingredients:

3 cups peeled, cored, chopped tomatoes

3 cups Hatch, Anaheim, or poblano chiles, chopped

¾ cup yellow onion, chopped

1 jalapeño pepper, seeded and finely chopped

6 cloves garlic, chopped

1½ cups vinegar (5%)

2 teaspoons ground cumin

1 teaspoon dried oregano leaf

1 teaspoon black pepper

1½ teaspoons salt

¼ cup finely chopped cilantro

Preparation: Combine first 10 ingredients in a large, non-reactive pot, such as stainless steel, and bring to a boil, stirring frequently. Reduce heat to medium and simmer 20–25 minutes. Remove salsa from heat and stir in chopped cilantro. (Stirring fresh cilantro in after cooking preserves the salsa's bright color.)

Ladle hot salsa into hot jars. Remove air bubbles; wipe jar rims. Cover at once with metal lids, and screw on rings until finger-tight. Process in a boiling-water canner for the appropriate time for your altitude. Remove and let cool for to 24 hours before labeling and storing.

SWEET ZUCCHINI RELISH

Makes approximately 5 pints

This recipe is a lifesaver when someone leaves a zucchini on the porch!
Coarsely chopping the zucchini creates a wonderful chunky-style relish.

Ingredients:

12 cups coarsely chopped zucchini
(about 12 medium)

4 cups chopped white onion

2 red bell peppers, seeded
and chopped

1 green bell pepper, seeded
and chopped

⅓ cup pickling salt

4 cups granulated sugar

2½ cups white distilled vinegar

2 tablespoons minced garlic

1 tablespoon ground turmeric

1 tablespoon black pepper

1½ teaspoons red pepper flakes

1 chopped chili pepper, with seeds

1 tablespoon salt

1 teaspoon dry mustard

Preparation: Combine zucchini, onions, bell peppers, and salt in a large glass or stainless steel bowl. Cover vegetables with a plate for added weight and let stand in refrigerator overnight.

Drain excess liquid from vegetables in bowl. Using your hands, press out additional liquid once more and drain from bowl. Add zucchini mixture, sugar, vinegar, garlic and next 6 ingredients in a large saucepan. Bring to a boil over medium-high heat, stirring occasionally. Reduce heat and simmer, stirring often or until liquid is reduced and mixture thickens (about 45 minutes). Keep hot.

Pour hot relish into hot jars, filling to ½ inch from top. Remove air bubbles; wipe jar rims. Cover at once with metal lids, and screw on rings until finger-tight. Process jars for the appropriate time for your altitude. Remove from hot water and let cool for up to 24 hours before labeling and storing.

THREE-INGREDIENT RASPBERRY JAM

Makes approximately 5 half-pint jars

No pectin is used in this recipe, which yields a wonderfully spreadable texture. It's pure raspberry flavor in a jar.

Ingredients:
4 cups fresh red raspberries
4 cups granulated sugar
4 tablespoons bottled lemon juice

Preparation: Pick raspberries over, removing stems and leaves. Mash raspberries, using a potato masher or a fork.

Bring mashed raspberries to a boil in a large saucepan; reduce heat, and simmer 5 minutes.

Add sugar and lemon juice to hot raspberries; bring to a boil, stirring constantly. Reduce heat, and simmer 5 minutes or until thickened. Jam has reached ideal thickness when it has a shiny appearance, and when hot liquid clings to a spoon. Keep hot.

Pour hot jam into hot jars. Remove air bubbles; wipe jar rims. Cover at once with metal lids, and screw on rings until finger-tight.

Process in a boiling-water bath for the appropriate time for your altitude, then remove and cool at room temperature up to 12 hours.

HEARTY MARINARA SAUCE

Makes approximately 9 pints

This hearty sauce is a versatile base for spaghetti, pizza sauce, and more.
(Note: *Don't adjust the proportions in the recipe below, which is based on USDA recommendations).*

Ingredients:

- 30 pounds tomatoes
- ¼ cup olive oil
- 1 cup chopped onion
- 5 cloves garlic, minced
- 1 cup chopped celery or green bell pepper
- 1 pound sliced fresh mushrooms (optional)
- 4½ teaspoons salt
- 2 tablespoons oregano
- 4 tablespoons minced parsley
- 2 teaspoons black pepper
- ¼ cup brown sugar

Preparation: Rinse and core fresh tomatoes. Blanch tomatoes in boiling water for 15 seconds and transfer into a bowl of ice water. Peel and discard skins. Working in batches, puree tomatoes in food processor until smooth. If you don't have a food processor, press unpeeled blanched tomatoes through a food mill or sieve into a bowl; discard skins. This may result in a chunkier texture.

Heat olive oil in the bottom of a large, non-reactive pot, such as stainless steel. Add onion, garlic, celery, and, if desired, mushrooms. Sauté over medium-high heat until just tender. Add tomatoes, salt, and next 4 ingredients to pot, and bring to a boil. Reduce heat and simmer 2 hours, stirring occasionally. Keep hot. Pour hot tomato sauce into hot jars, filling to ½ inch from top. Remove air bubbles; wipe jar rims. Cover at once with metal lids, and screw on rings until finger-tight. Process using the appropriate time and PSI for your altitude and type of canner.

CANNING POPULAR VEGETABLES

For best quality, use vegetables that are ripe and unblemished. If you are unable to can on the day the vegetables are harvested, they should be refrigerated until use. It is not necessary to add salt to canned vegetables, except for flavor. You may use hot cooking liquid, rather than draining vegetables and adding new boiling water. Using the liquid that the vegetables are cooked in creates better flavor. About 20 pounds of unhusked corn will yield about 9 pints of canned product. Select firm, unblemished ears of corn.

CANNED SWEET CORN

Makes approximately 9 pints

Preparation: Husk corn, remove silks and rinse. Boil ears of corn about 3 minutes, then let cool. Cut cooked kernels from cob, using a large kitchen knife.

Safety Tip: When cutting corn from the cob, stand each ear of corn on its base, on a cutting board. Hold the corn near its top, then cut downward slowly, until all corn is removed.

Place corn kernels in a large saucepan with 1 cup clean water per each quart of kernels. Bring to a boil; reduce heat, and simmer 5 minutes. Keep hot.

Pack corn and hot liquid in hot jars, filling to 1 inch from top. Remove air bubbles; wipe jar rims. Cover at once with metal lids, and screw on rings until finger-tight. Process using the appropriate time and PSI for your altitude.

CANNED PEAS

Makes approximately 6 pints

Canning your own sweet peas at home will change your mind about canned peas forever! Canned peas benefit from light seasoning, so we have added a pinch of salt to this recipe for best results. Approximately 13.5 pounds of fresh, shelled peas will yield about 6 pints of canned product.

Ingredients:
13.5 pounds fresh, unshelled peas
½ teaspoon kosher or other
    high-quality salt per jar to
    be canned
1 gallon clean, fresh water

Preparation: Shell and lightly rinse peas. Bring water to a boil in a large saucepan.

Add ½ teaspoon salt to each hot jar. Loosely pack raw peas in hot jars, filling to 1 inch from top. Cover peas with boiling water, filling to 1 inch from top. Remove air bubbles; wipe jar rims. Cover at once with metal lids, and screw on rings until finger-tight. Process according to the appropriate time and PSI for your altitude and canner.

CANNED CARROTS

Makes approximately 6 pints

The smaller the better! Canned carrots will have the best taste and texture if larger, more fibrous ones are not used. Approximately 7.5 pounds of fresh carrots will yield about 6 pint jars of canned product.

Preparation: Wash and peel carrots, and rinse to remove scraps.

Slice carrots into small rounds or cubes, discarding tips and ends.

Place carrots in a saucepan, and cover with water. Bring to a boil; reduce heat to medium, and simmer 5 minutes.

Ladle cooked carrots and hot liquid into hot jars, filling to 1 inch from top. Remove air bubbles; wipe jar rims. Cover at once with metal lids, and screw on rings until finger-tight.

Process according to the appropriate time and PSI for your altitude and canner.

CANNED SMOKED FISH

You'll need ⅔ of a pound of smoked fish for each pint

Using pressure canning also helps to destroy lingering bacteria that may remain after the smoking process. **Safety note:** *A canner no less than 16 quart-size should be used; before canning any fish, ensure that it has been properly smoked.*

This recipe is adapted from Canning Smoked Fish At Home *by Barbara Rasco, Carolyn Raab, and Sandra McCurdy, University of Idaho Extension.*

Preparation: When preparing smoked fish, only prepare as much as you are able to can in a day. Only half-pint or pint jars should be used, as safe processing times are calibrated to these volumes. Smoked fish that has been frozen can be processed using this method.

Thaw frozen product in the refrigerator (never at room temperature!) until fully thawed and without ice crystals. You may use this method to can smoked fish that has previously been vacuum-sealed and frozen as well. Pack thawed smoked fish into each jar, filling 1 inch between pieces and from top of jar. Do not add liquid!

Smoked fish can be oily. Wipe jar rims to remove any oily residue. Cover at once with metal lids, and screw on rings until finger-tight. Measure 4 quarts (16 cups) of cool tap water and pour into the pressure canner. Don't decrease the water amount or heat it before processing. Process according to the appropriate time and PSI for your altitude and canner.

Always store smoked fish in cool, dry places away from direct sunlight and without risk of freezing. It is of utmost importance that canned, smoked fish be consumed within 1 calendar year. Remember to carefully inspect your jars after canning and before opening or eating.

SWEET POTATOES IN LIGHT SYRUP

Makes approximately 9 pints

When canning potatoes, do not use the water in which you have cooked them to also fill your jars! Always use new, fresh water to fill jars, to avoid extra starch in your final product.

Ingredients:

11 pounds fresh sweet potatoes
  (small to medium)

1 teaspoon salt per each jar to
  be canned

To make light syrup:

6½ cups water

¾ cup granulated sugar

Preparation: Gently wash sweet potatoes. Combine sweet potatoes and water to cover in a large pot; bring to a boil, and cook 15-20 minutes or until partially soft. Completely drain cooking water. Let sweet potatoes cool before handling.

Peel off and discard skins. Cut potatoes into even pieces or rounds, so that pieces will fit neatly into jars. Do not mash or otherwise break down pieces. Overhandling sweet potatoes will release excess starch, clouding your final product. Pack potato pieces in hot jars, filling to 1 inch from top. Sprinkle 1 teaspoon salt over sweet potatoes in each jar.

Combine water and sugar in a saucepan over low to medium heat; heat, stirring constantly, until sugar dissolves. Keep syrup hot. Cover sweet potatoes with hot syrup, filling to 1 inch from top. Remove air bubbles; wipe jar rims. Cover at once with metal lids, and screw on rings until finger-tight. Process according to the appropriate time and PSI for your altitude and canner.

WHITE POTATOES
Makes approximately 9 pints

Can your own white or russet potatoes, then add directly to pot pies, stews, soups, and other dishes. Or drain, heat, and mash for quick and easy mashed potatoes any time! Approximately 13 pounds of fresh potatoes yields 9 pints of canned product. Small potatoes may be canned whole, while medium to larger-size ones should be cut or cubed first.

Preparation: Wash and peel potatoes. If desired, cut into cubes. Combine potato cubes and water to cover in a large pot; bring to a boil, and cook 2–3 minutes or until just soft. (Cook whole potatoes up to 10 minutes.) Completely drain cooking water.

Bring more water to a boil, enough to fill jars.

Loosely pack hot potatoes in hot jars, filling to 1 inch from top. Cover potato tops with boiling water, filling to 1 inch from top. Remove air bubbles; wipe jar rims. Cover at once with metal lids, and screw on rings until finger-tight.

Process for the appropriate time and PSI for your altitude and canner.

PROCESS TIMES BY CANNING METHOD AND ELEVATION

PROCESS TIMES WITH A BOILING-WATER CANNER

RECIPE	JAR SIZE	MY ELEVATION IS (in feet)		
		1,000	1,001–6,000	>6,000 lower
Easy Apple Butter	Quart	10 min.	15 min.	20 min.
Easy Dill Pickles	Pint	10 min.	15 min.	20 min.
	Quart	15 min.	20 min.	25 min.
Blueberry Jam	Pint	10 min.	10 min.	15 min.
Canned Peaches	Pint	20 min.	30 min.	35 min.
	Quart	25 min.	35 min.	40 min.
Pickled Beets	Pint	30 min.	40 min.	45 min.
Best Game Day Salsa	Pint	15 min.	20 min.	25 min.
Sweet Zucchini Relish	Pint	15 min.	25 min.	30 min.
Three-ingredient Raspberry Jam	Half-pint	10 min.	10 min.	15 min.

PROCESS TIMES WITH A DIAL-GAUGE PRESSURE CANNER

RECIPE	JAR SIZE	PROCESS TIME (in minutes)	MY ELEVATION IS (in feet)			
			0–2,000	2,001–4,000	4,001–6,000	6,001–8,000
Hearty Marinara Sauce	Pint	20	11 PSI	12 PSI	13 PSI	14 PSI
	Quart	25	11 PSI	12 PSI	13 PSI	14 PSI
Canned Sweet Corn	Pint	55	11 PSI	12 PSI	13 PSI	14 PSI
	Quart	85	11 PSI	12 PSI	13 PSI	14 PSI
Canned Peas	Pint or Quart	40	11 PSI	12 PSI	13 PSI	14 PSI
Canned Carrots	Pint	25	11 PSI	12 PSI	13 PSI	14 PSI
	Quart	30	11 PSI	12 PSI	13 PSI	14 PSI
Canned Smoked Fish	Half-pint or Pint	110	11 PSI	12 PSI	13 PSI	14 PSI
Sweet Potatoes in Light Syrup	Pint	65	11 PSI	12 PSI	13 PSI	14 PSI
	Quart	90	11 PSI	12 PSI	13 PSI	14 PSI
White Potatoes	Pint	35	11 PSI	12 PSI	13 PSI	14 PSI
	Quart	40	11 PSI	12 PSI	13 PSI	14 PSI

PROCESS TIMES WITH A WEIGHTED-GAUGE PRESSURE CANNER

RECIPE	JAR SIZE	PROCESS TIME (in minutes)	MY ELEVATION IS (in feet)	
			0–1,000	Above 1,000
Hearty Marinara Sauce	Pint	20	10 lb.	15 lb.
	Quart	25	10 lb.	15 lb.
Canned Sweet Corn	Pint	55	10 lb.	15 lb.
	Quart	85	10 lb.	15 lb.
Canned Peas	Pint or Quart	40	10 lb.	15 lb.
Canned Carrots	Pint	25	10 lb.	15 lb.
	Quart	30	10 lb.	15 lb.
Canned Smoked Fish	Half-pint or Pint	110	10 lb.	15 lb.
Sweet Potatoes in Light Syrup	Pint	65	10 lb.	15 lb.
	Quart	90	10 lb.	15 lb.
White Potatoes	Pint	35	10 lb.	15 lb.
	Quart	40	10 lb.	15 lb.

Enjoy the Bounties of Summer and Autumn All Year Long

Learn the skills of canning and preserving, and savor those fresh flavors any time you choose

Easy-to-follow booklet of photo-illustrated instructions for gardeners, foragers, and anyone who enjoys fresh produce

- Introduction to the basics of canning and preserving popular foods
- Step-by-step guide to boiling-water canning and pressure canning—with 15 recipes in all
- Food warnings, safety precautions, and equipment needed
- Information about storing and using your preserves
- Expert author with a lifetime of experience

Collect all the Adventure Skills Guides

ISBN 978-1-59193-943-6 **$9.95**